JOURNEY *of the*

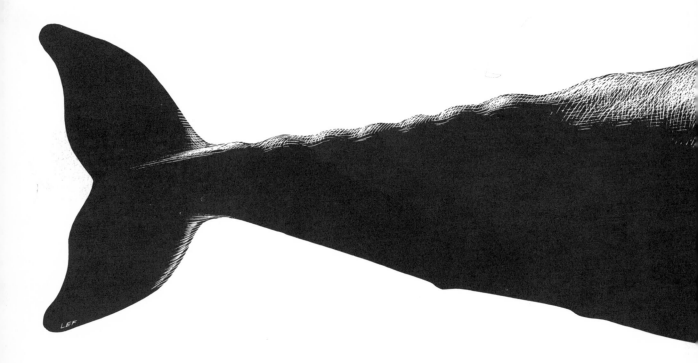

GRAY WHALES

by GLADYS CONKLIN

illustrated by LEONARD EVERETT FISHER

HOLIDAY HOUSE · NEW YORK

Dedicated to
Jacques-Yves Cousteau
and his devoted crew who are bringing
to us the wonders of the mysterious ocean

"The whale that our team has the greatest affection
for is the gray whale of California, with whom we
lived for several months."
—*The Whale, Mighty Monarch of the Sea*
by Jacques-Yves Cousteau
and Philippe Diolé

Text copyright © 1974 by Gladys Conklin
Illustrations copyright © 1974 by Leonard Everett Fisher
All rights reserved
Printed in the United States of America

LIBRARY OF CONGRESS CATALOGING IN PUBLICATION DATA

Conklin, Gladys Plemon.
    Journey of the gray whales.
    SUMMARY: Follows the activities of a mother whale
and her calf from the latter's birth to his weaning as
they migrate up the California coast to the Bering Sea.
    1.   Pacific gray whale—Juvenile literature.
[1.   Pacific gray whale.   2.   Whales]   I.   Fisher,
Leonard Everett, illus.   II.   Title.
QL737.C425C66   599'.51   74-5445
ISBN 0-8234-0244-4

Author's Note

The migration of the California gray whale along the Pacific Coast is called the "Moby Dick Parade." Thousands of people gather on the headlands to watch the whales. The California coast is the only place in the world where so many whales can be seen so close to land. They may be seen rolling in the surf, "treading water" on their tails, or floating in the water taking naps.

In San Diego and Los Angeles harbors, excursion boats have regular schedules for taking visitors out for a two-hour trip right into the midst of the whales. This water excursion is the prize field trip of the year for many school children.

Whales are divided into two orders according to their feeding habits: the toothed whales and the toothless, or baleen, whales. Toothed whales eat almost anything alive that they can catch, from the small sardine to the mighty squid. The baleen whales are bottom-feeders, scooping up small shellfish and clams.

The gray whale of California, *Eschrichtius glaucus*, is a baleen whale. Its upper jaw is lined on each side with two rows of horny plates hung with a thick mat of fibers. These fibers act as a sieve to strain and hold the food as the water runs out of the whale's mouth.

A few men have made a serious study of the gray whale. The author is deeply indebted to the following:

The Life History and Ecology of the Gray Whale, by Dale W. Rice and Allen A. Wolman (American Society of Mammalogists, 1971)

The Marine Mammals of the Northwestern Coast of North America, by Charles M. Scammon (Putnam, 1874, and Dover Publications, 1968)

The Whale, Mighty Monarch of the Sea, by Jacques-Yves Cousteau and Philippe Diolé (Doubleday, 1972)

Huge dark shapes disturbed the quiet waters of the lagoon on this December day. The shiny, dark forms moved through the water half submerged. Two thousand gray whales were returning to the warm waters where they were born. This was the thirty-five-mile-long Scammon Lagoon in Baja California, Mexico.

As the rising sun cast the first sparkle upon the
water, the noisy activity in the lagoon increased.
A teeming, surging mass of whales seemed to fill the
area. The air was full of misty sprays as huge blackish
bodies came to the surface to blow and sent a long low
whoooosh sound rolling across the water. As they
went under again, there was the thundering
crash of their flukes, the horizontal tail fins.

This was the time and place for giving birth to the young. A cow whale was steadily making her way toward the far end of the lagoon where the males never came. The cow seemed to be in distress as she humped her back and twisted from side to side. Her massive body was swollen with a new calf that had been growing inside her for nearly a year. Another female was with her, a "helper" whale, which slowly circled around her to keep other whales from coming too close.

When the birth time arrived, the infant whale came tail
first from the mother's body. If an infant came
head first, it might drown before it could get its
first breath of air. Whales have lungs to breathe
with, so the newborn calf had to get to the surface
quickly. When it was free of the mother's body,
both the mother and the helper gently pushed the
sixteen-foot-long calf up to the surface.

Then the mother let his head sink below the surface
and quickly pushed it up again. She repeated this
raising and lowering in the water over and over
until the calf had learned to breathe. A whale's
nostrils, called blowholes, are on the top of its
head. Some whales have one blowhole but the gray
whales have two. A new calf must learn to keep its
blowholes tightly closed when it goes under water, or it
will choke on the sea water that would trickle
down its throat.

The mother stayed at the surface and turned on
her side. This brought her nipples to the water's
edge so the calf could nurse and breathe at the same
time. There were two nipples, partly hidden in a fold
of the skin on either side of her abdomen. The calf
pushed around his mother's body until he found a
soft spot that fitted his mouth, then he pressed hard.

A special muscle squirted a strong stream of milk into the back of his throat. The milk was yellow and very rich and the calf drank a gallon or two at each feeding. As he nursed, the mother held him in place with her flippers.

While the pregnant females were giving birth to
their young in the quiet areas of the lagoon, the
large open areas were full of commotion as the males tried
to mate with other females. Mating in the
water was a long and difficult process for
these huge animals. After a male found a willing mate,
there was a great deal of action and splashing in the
water until the two got into a satisfactory position.

They lay on their sides facing each other. The female grasped the male with her flippers to help keep their position. There was also a breathing problem that increased the difficulty of the mating—they must both be ready to come to the surface to breathe at the same time. It took many attempts before the pair coupled satisfactorily.

One morning there was a feeling of restlessness
in the lagoon. Whales began swimming up and down
through the center channel. Suddenly a big bull
whale lifted his flukes high, brought them down with
a thundering smash, and headed for the mouth of
the lagoon.

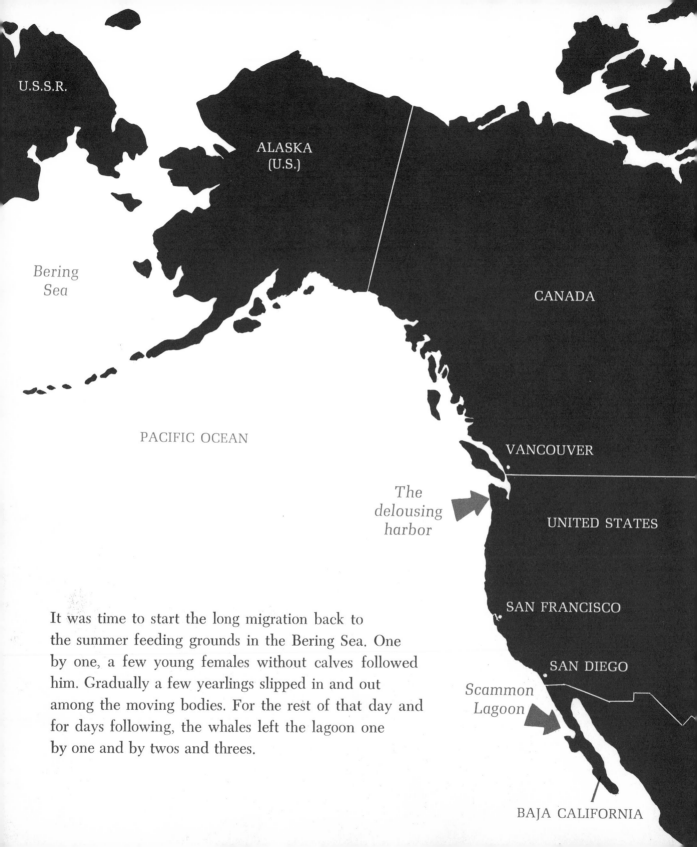

U.S.S.R.

ALASKA
(U.S.)

Bering
Sea

CANADA

PACIFIC OCEAN

VANCOUVER

The
delousing
harbor

UNITED STATES

SAN FRANCISCO

It was time to start the long migration back to
the summer feeding grounds in the Bering Sea. One
by one, a few young females without calves followed
him. Gradually a few yearlings slipped in and out
among the moving bodies. For the rest of that day and
for days following, the whales left the lagoon one
by one and by twos and threes.

SAN DIEGO

Scammon
Lagoon

BAJA CALIFORNIA

The young calf and his mother, with the helper close behind, were among the last to leave the lagoon. The calf weighed about 1000 pounds on the day that he was born. His mother's milk was so rich that he gained about 230 pounds a day. His layer of blubber, or fat, was a thick blanket around him and would keep him warm in the icy waters where he would spend the summer months.

If any danger threatened, the two cows would keep
the calf between them as they traveled near the coast.
The only enemy that they feared was the killer whale.
The killers are small whales that travel in packs and
are bloodthirsty animals in their endless search for
food. A healthy gray whale can usually defend itself
from the killers but a mother with a young calf must
always be on guard against them.

With the calf safely between them, the cow whale and
her helper entered the vast, uncertain ocean. There
was no sign of other whales. Gray whales don't travel
in large groups. There may be two together or
three, but usually each whale travels by itself.

The calf was still a beginner at swimming and the mother slowed down so that he might keep up with her. His speed would increase day by day. The mother swam steadily with a slow, smooth beat of her flukes up and down. She often stayed underwater for eight or ten minutes at a time.

When the calf was hungry, he swam close to his mother's
side, almost touching her. When she ignored him,
he would poke her with his head and even slam his
body against her side. Soon she would slow down and
turn over for him to nurse.

One clear morning, when the water was smooth, with
not a whitecap in sight, a pack of
killer whales appeared. Their black, shiny dorsal fins stood
six feet high as they cut through the calm water at top
speed. Killers roamed far over the seas, always
eager to fight and eat any animal available. Each killer
was armed with a mouthful of forty or more sharply
pointed teeth. The gray whale had only one weapon, but a
powerful one. It was the pair of huge flukes of her tail.

Quickly the cow and her helper got the calf safely between them. Almost at once they were surrounded by biting, darting killers as the water was churned into white foam. Twisting and curving around the calf to keep him protected, the two females fought back.

As they turned and twisted, their mighty flukes seemed
to be everywhere. A killer darted in and nicked the
mother's tail. In a flash, she raised her flukes high
and smashed them down on the back of the killer, putting
an end to his activity. The other killers tried to
reach the calf, which was really what they wanted, but the
bodies of the two cows were always shielding him.

Finally the powerful flukes struck the head of a
killer with a shattering blow. As the killer rolled
over on his back, the water turned red. The blood
aroused the other killers—they turned on
their crippled companion and started tearing the
body to pieces.

The two females and the calf made a quick dive and disappeared. When they reached a small, sheltered bay, the mother turned in to rest in the quiet water and to let the calf nurse. When he had finished, she felt the need for food. The helper stayed with the calf while the mother sank to the bottom and scooped up barrelfuls of tiny clams and shellfish.

The three continued on their way up the coast. Each day was about the same. They swam with their heads underwater, surfaced to blow and fill their lungs with fresh air, sank again, and went on swimming. There were frequent stops to let the calf nurse.

One morning dawned with a difference that disturbed
the calf. A strong wind was sending big waves rolling
toward the beach while a pelting rain was making
saucers on the surface of the water. This was the
calf's first experience with raindrops and giant waves.
He didn't like them. He swam underneath his mother's body
and she slowed to keep him covered.

Later that day they came to a harbor entrance where a river emptied into the ocean. Many of the gray whales stopped at this place on their way north. The water was shallow and the bottom of the harbor was heavily graveled. As the two cows turned into the harbor entrance, they found a few of their lagoon companions there.

The calf stayed near the surface while the two females
sank to the bottom. There they rolled and twisted,
rubbing their bellies hard on the gravel to remove the
soft, clinging whale lice that they had picked up in the
warm waters of Baja California. Their bodies were
covered with barnacles, too. These would drop
off as the whales entered the colder waters of the north.

It is the barnacles that give the gray whale its name. The gray whale is really black in color but the many barnacles on its body leave white scars when they drop off or are rubbed off. This gives the whale a mottled gray appearance.

The irritating reddish lice had gathered in thick clusters around
the barnacles. For long minutes the whales worked hard,
squashing and rubbing off the lice and some of the barnacles.
When they could wait no longer, a powerful thrust of
their bodies sent them up to the surface for fresh air.
Opening both blowholes, they sent huge spouts spraying up
as high as fifteen feet. There were ten or twelve spouts
all over the area at the same time.

The harbor was also a place for play. Gray whales
like to dive in and out of big waves and roll in the
surf. The young calves played in the kelp. They dived
under large masses of the slippery brown ribbons of seaweed
and came up with their bodies covered with long strands.
These would slowly slip along their backs and fall off.
Again and again they dived down under the floating sea
garden and popped up again dripping with the soft plants.

Suddenly a huge body shot straight up out of the water
until the black head and small eyes were well
above the surface. The whale was actually standing on its
tail. It was able to keep this balance for one full minute.
Another whale playfully burst out of the water at great speed,
rolled over, and crashed again into the water
on its back with a tremendous splash.

For a few days the whales fed,
tried to get rid of their lice, and then moved on
toward the Bering Sea. When they arrived there,
the calf had successfully finished the longest
migration made by any mammal. Here he had
one more important thing to learn.

When his mother went down to the bottom to feed, he
went with her. He watched her open her huge mouth and
scoop up tiny shrimps and crabs, along with water and
sand. The baleen, or whalebone, in her mouth held back
the food as the water and sand ran out. Again and
again she filled her mouth until she had swallowed
about 300 pounds of the small crustaceans.

The calf learned by watching, but he wasn't interested in trying his mother's food. He was still nursing and would continue to nurse for another five or six months. He would be weaned about the time that the whales started south again for the winter.

One day, much later, his mother came near but he
didn't stir. For the first time in his life
he had no urge for a drink of milk. Instead he sank
to the bottom and scooped up shrimps and crabs till he
could eat no more. He came to the surface and floated,
his hunger satisfied. Now the calf was weaned.
He was becoming an adult at last.

Glossary

baleen, or *whalebone*: a horny substance in two rows of plates hanging from the upper jaw of baleen whales

blow: the action of the whale to expel moist air from the blowhole

blowhole: a nostril in the top of the head of a whale

blubber: the fat of whales

crustacean: a class of sea life including shrimps, crabs, and barnacles

dorsal fin: a fin situated near or on the back of an animal

flukes: the rounded projections of a whale's tail

lagoon: an area of shallow water separated from the ocean by low banks

spout: the column of spray or vapor sent from the blowhole of a whale

Index